A Thousand Bullets

A Thousand Bullets Gone Astray

Clay Lowe

58K
fifty eight kings press

With thanks to: Richard Watson, Sean Kelly, Torrance Stephens Cathy Kunst, Linda Baker and the Pure and Good and Right open mic poetry club

First published in the Great Britain in 2009 by
fifty eight kings press
3 Mayfield Road, Southam CV47 0JX

Copyright © Clay Lowe 2009

Clay Lowe has asserted his moral rights in accordance with the Copyright, Designs and Patents Act of 1988.

ISBN 978-0-9561250-1-9

For Ruth

A musician must make music, an artist must paint, a poet must write, if he is to be at peace with himself. What a man can be he must be. This is the need we may call self-actualization. - DR Abraham Maslow

Contents

1. Promises 11
stiffed 12
dead poets 14
all the paths I could travel 18
dying in my tv chair 20
on the edge of forever 22
when ravens cry 24
what's that I hear? 27
shakespeare and vermouth 29
2. A Love Story 31
janine 32
kindred spirits 34
perfume 36
forgotten love 37
white sheets 39
if i could 41
white-hot poker 42
mistress 43
cherry pants 45
her dreams have all gone to bed 48
i thought you should know 50
oblivion 52

3. A Day in the Life	57
my mother	58
behind enemy lines	59
the Word	60
on meeting my muse	62
people want to put me	64
a crack in the revolution	66
chemical attraction	69
flight attendant	71
uber cool	73
american girl	74
beast barracks	76
is this the one	78
junk mail	79
how sweet she might smell	81
dr earnest and professor b	83
jane doe	86
song of my ancestors	90
4. Whiskey Shots	93
torture	94
death part I	95
i think, therefore	96
echo	97
dawn	98

the shakes	99
coffee	100
self-portrait	101
death part II	102
listen	103
5. A World Gone Mad	105
turn the page	106
stand together	109
the guru	111
prophet man	113

1. Promises

stiffed

Those who would be your master
Pick upon the bones of your disaster
While you lie awake and worry
They plot and scheme and scurry

About looking for next weeks news
They amuse themselves with statistics
The police are checking the ballistics
Of a thousand bullets gone astray
And you pray between shots of whiskey and blues

Tomorrow will be a better day
At least that's what the weathermen say
Meanwhile you wiggle in wretched sheets
Struggling to make ends meet
You hope there is a better way

To live a life of sound and fury
Let the jury judge your works of passion
While you keep up with the latest fashion
The time you thought you had tomorrow

Disappears beneath tears and sorrow

As you dance to a beat not your own
You hear the rhythm of your heart...beat
moan

dead poets

I had promise you know
I learned to love the literature
of men whose words had power
who could sing to a Grecian Urn
or make Ozymandias' broken stones
immortal

Yes my heart leapt up
when I first read
the rainbow in the sky
and the lady who walks
in the beauty of the night
where truth is beauty
and beauty truth

Their voices, now, quiet and dim
drowned by the din of little men
little men who traded:
courage for contentment
passion for passiveness
surprise for sensibility

In the din they screamed,
dare to dream, but don't dream too far
stay on par with the crowd,
with the hive of little men

And the dead poets go:
Rage, rage against the smothering of your
light

The time of the poet is past
haven't you read, the form is dead
drowned out by the drumbeats
of modern feats the square box
filled with straw fills the head of the
walking dead, who, tired and uninspired
drag themselves from space to space
killing time between the dashes
until their bodies are laid to rest in ashes

I wiggle with Sweeny among the
nightingales
my tales held close inside
they (that is the mythical they)
took me aside and in their wrath

taught me the ways of wine, women and
war

I counted the days to my release
but soon found to my dismay
the outside is the same as the inside
only no one to salute and the mantra
duty, honor, country dubbed over with
increase profits and shareholder value

And the dead poets go:
Rage, rage against the smothering of your
light

Years pass, the idealism of my youth
trodden
under muddy boots and pinstriped suits
the labour of my work fruit-less, or so it
seemed

until I came upon a woods,
a place I had known before
a path, two choices, which way to go
I heard the dead poets laugh
The choices we chose are half chance

it is all but a dream within a dream
from which we wake and lie drowning

all the paths I could travel

All the paths I could
travel are pointing me
in 360 directions

Which path I choose
is hard for me
to imagine.

If I move in one direction
the circle collapses and
my path becomes fixed

I can't help but wonder
what would happen if
I chose another path

Where would that one lead me
What would I be giving up
What would I become?

You can be or do anything
you want, so the words go

and that's true.

The problem isn't lack
of choice; it's too much
choice that spends my head

Which path to choose I
cannot tell, so I stand still
keeping the circle in tact.

dying in my tv chair

Promises made
Promises kept
Never this way was it meant
To be

Dying here
Dying there
My dreams have gone nowhere

Hard work
Work hard
Success will be yours

Mrs Fader said.

She lied or didn't tell the truth
standing up there in front of the class with
her pea green skirt (hanging just below her
knees)
not long enough to save us
from her ugly varicose veins!

Mrs Fader

The world isn't as you said
the streets are made of lead
no gold in sight

Hard work
Broken back
A trailer and two rug rats

Promises made
Promises kept
A big legged woman on my back

Dying here
Dying there
Dying in my TV chair

on the edge of forever

The world is closing in
I cannot see the sky. Trapped
like the wings of a butterfly between
the fingers of little boys.

The Shadow lingers waiting for me to falter,
and like the panther waiting in the wings,
dark and sullen, stands ready to pounce
and rip the bones from my flesh

I question the darkness,
but no counsel hear.
Voices sing up from the river
drawing me near like the siren's song

I wander across the Plains of Moab.
I hear the trumpets sound.
The people kneel before the sullen
Priests and stare.

They cannot shout for me
my soul is too black, and the space

between the dark and the light
is too wide for me to cross.

I pray for the voices to wake me before
I drown, but in the darkness there is no
One to hear the sound that dribbles
from my parched lips in broken prayer.

when ravens cry
      To J.

You are a raven
against a blank sky

The earth hides her colors
from you while you hide
your true Self from her

Your soul sighs behind a
prison of your own making
pacing back and forth

In your tired eyes I see
a prisoner, wrongly imprisoned
crying out for freedom

Your soul's cry falls on
deaf ears in the silence
of your eyes

The ravens gather in the fields
under grey skies they come
to hear your soul's lament:

Oh please set me free
Let me walk through the fields
In bare feet, my arms wide open
Embracing the sun

The ravens bow their heads
they know permission
will not come

Until the best part
of your youth and strength
have passed away

and your limbs have
gone to sleep; your
spirit deflated

Because it knows you
could have been great had
you acted without permission

And set your soul free
to be alive, to be wild,
to wander and enjoy life

for life's own sake

Greatness is not so rare
but rare is the courage
to live life full of
passion and grace

The ravens fly
away one by one
against a blank sky

what's that I hear?

time, that beautiful handmaiden
whispered in my ear:

you gotta get going baby
you gotta get going
death is near

but i've got songs to write
sweet melodic words to pen
surely it must be a sin
to die with them within?

then you gotta write baby
you gotta write
get those words down on a page
act them out on the stage

oh time, my sweet, won't
you love me more?
i'll pen a phrase, turn a word or two
in honour of your amour

i can't baby i can't
you have what time you have
and no more

(knock, knock)

what's that i hear?

tis death knocking at the door

shakespeare and vermouth

My path diverted from my youth,
coerced to do minor work
a pack mule on a mountain trail
no time for Shakespeare and vermouth

There's no future in poetry
it's all push button proz-ac
a co-dead sign for the new wise
worn like a night time accessory

I chase my passion at my own risk
(the safe bet is with my nine to five) can't
contain my pleasure measure for measure
on that new gazillion gig hard disc

Give me Byron, Shelly, and Frost
set my soul on fire and my hair too
back on purpose with my passion
forget the machine and the boss

2. A Love Story

janine

Janine, my dream, I want to drink you up
like a Kasteel Cru on a lonely night

Like the night we first met
I was passing through without a lot to do.
You were behind the desk on the headset
While Benny Goodman played Roll 'em on the clarinet
I was dreaming of nothing until I walked into you

Janine, my dream, I want to drink you up
like a Kasteel Cru on a lonely night

I couldn't escape your soft brown eyes
They held me in place transfixed, mesmerized
Like a cool mountain lake on a hot summer day
I wanted to dive right into you
Lost forever in your eyes

Janine, my dream, I want to drink you up
like a Kasteel Cru on a lonely night

I want to wrap myself up in your smile
I'd tell you that I love you, but how could I reconcile
The distance between the mile I'd have to crawl
To cross the divide between the real and imagined
How could I ever tell you how I feel?

Janine, my dream, I want to drink you up
like a Kasteel Cru on a lonely night

kindred spirits

You opened the door to
your heart and I stepped
through to warm my bones
beside your fire

To love you was easy
from the moment we met
a kindred spirit of innocent
intent. You spoke a word

or two as people do when
meeting someone new. Your
words were like an incantation
setting my soul afire

You are my safe harbor
my port against the storm
a place where I can hide
my confessions and confide
my hopes and dreams.

I'm glad you showed up

with your open door so
we could dance in the clouds
and drink from the summer rain.

perfume

I carry the smell
of your perfume

           lingering

around me as I walk
a mile from our house

I carry you with me
through savage streets

           clinging

to the knowledge someone
somewhere loves me

or so I thought

forgotten love

Have we forgotten
Forgotten how to be romantic?
Sick with puppy-love

I want to return
Return to the warmth of your embrace.
Are you waiting for my return?
I return,
We talk of things functional;
    carpets;
        school plays;
            kitchen fittings.

Have we forgotten
Forgotten how to be romantic?
Sick with puppy-love

Maybe it's my fault
My fault;
I spend too much time in my own head
I used to never leave the house
Without kissing you

Kissing you;
    on the carpet;
        in the back of the stands;
            in the kitchen.

Have we forgotten
Forgotten how to be romantic?
Sick with puppy-love

white sheets

We talk of time and things dear
your breast half-exposed untouched
but dreadfully near

The dawn beckons something new
taunting, teasing, tempting
me away from the comfort

of our white sheets
a thousand times I've
turned away from your familiar

touch grown cold.
A strand of hair falls
across your tired face

I reach; you pull
we bend and twist
in our white sheets

Never coming closer
than the space between

our pillows

if i could

If I could but pull you close
to whisper in your ear
a thousands thoughts
of things dear.

A tremor in my heart
no veil to conceal
the truth of my soul's desire
a secret love I long to reveal.

If time should pass
this moment gone
keep close my words
let them linger on.

white-hot poker

A cacophony of emotions
Danced the tango in my head
A vow un-wed
In my head a thousand times a day
Stunned confusion
Like a white-hot poker
Driven over and
Over in my poor... little... head

mistress

Have you not felt the gentle
Caress of words, softly spoken,
That stroke the fibers of your soul
Like the tender touch of a lover

Touching you in that place
That makes your body shake
Like the tremor of an earthquake.

Your beauty radiates across
A crowded room like an irresistible
Beacon of desire, drawing those
Near who long to grasp
The eternal mystery of the world

Yet you cannot hear the soft
Sound of poetry whispered in your ear

A sound that soothes the soul
And makes the heart beat
Like a thousand shamans' drums

Beating a rhythmic beat of
Exotic journeys told
Through words, ideas are felt
Through words, shaped inside a poem,
Love is won and love is lost
Nations rise and fall

Through words a poet can
Make you laugh or cry

A poem is like a lover's touch
Taking you to places you
Did not know you could go.

cherry pants

My mind is
fair to mild
this morning I
sense a storm
forming
thunder hides the conflict
in my head
lightening reveals
her cherry
red pants on my bed
quietly she stands
misunderstood
a rebel between causes
she pauses
but does not
stop
to think
why
I could not die
for the stars
on her back

her love is
like sugar free tv

She spends her days
in pajamas
acting out tv
dramas
her mama's yelling
up the stairs
to get a
life
she tells me
some days she wishes
she could
die

I push her
up against
the wall
and kiss her
like I mean it
Her cherry red
pants
have me entranced
but like the men in

Holytown I can't
pin her down
she laughs
because she knows

her love is like
sugar free tv

her dreams have all gone to bed

The wind whispers between
raindrops of yesterday's past
the memory of her last kiss
fades to black

She can see her happiness
stagger out the front door
into the arms of another
perfumed night

Her broken dreams have
all gone to bed haunted by
ghosts of lines left unsaid

In the morning she can see
the sun hanging wearily on the
horizon, casting empty shadows
on the pillow by her head

She can feel the emptiness
swim around inside her as
she drags herself out of bed

In the mirror she catches
her reflection, smeared mascara
underneath her brown eyes

She can spend another day
holding hands with the past
pretending everything is ok

She can hear the wind between
the raindrops and she wonders
how long can it last?

i thought you should know

I'm your lover when I'm not
Busy hating you for making me feel
Small like the fly you flicked the other
Day because it landed near your plate

I'm a man when I'm not being
Castrated by your bored look as
You turn on the light to go wash me
Off of you like you did after you petted
That stray dog the other day

I'm forgiving when I'm not being vengeful
Thinking about the best way to hurt you
Like I did the other day when I told
You how your clothes don't fit any more
And wearing black doesn't make you look
thin

I'm happy when I'm not being sad
Watching you walk out the house like
You did the other day to go be a whore
As if I didn't know his name is Richard

It says so on the card you dropped on the
floor

I'm kind when I'm not being cruel
Like when I fingered your sister in the
Bathroom the other day while you were
Downstairs talking to her boyfriend and
Cooking dinner for the four of us to enjoy

oblivion

Old man saddles
up to the bar
says I need a
liquid transfusion
of your best cold
stuff

It's the image
of her eyes
filled up to despise
all the stupid
little things I've
done

I'm haunted by
the sounds of
her sobs in the
dark when she
thinks I'm still
asleep

I stare at the

ceiling and the
cracks in the wall
and I wonder how
we ever even
ended up like this

I can remember
a time when
your eyes shone
bright in the
sunlight on the
arms of the
Park St bridge

You whispered in
my ears, sweet
nothings and that
was fine, cause
i could smell your
perfume and feel
your breasts against
my chest and your
warm slender
fingers tied up
between strokes

of your hair

Now I sit in
this bar after
midnight choking
on the crusts
of your despair
sipping MGD and
getting high on
Saul Williams

And I long for
the time when
you were there
beside me feeding
me lines from
his book

I'm a low flying
crook who
swooped down on
your heart, carried
it to heights
then smashed it
on the rocks

below

And I watched
your broken dreams
crumble and get
mixed up in the
sand and washed
away in the sea

floating in the
night like a
piece of dead
wood drifting
to be washed
up on the banks
of Babylon

a city in strife
like your broken
heart mourning
lost in oblivion

3. A Day in the Life

my mother

Child of Aquarius
loved funkadelic music
moonbeams and magic

She took care of us
kept us fed, watered
and warm at night

Taught us the difference
between wrong and right
Use your head she said

don't be nobody's fool
depend on yourself and
yourself alone, others will

let you down as
sure as the sun
follows the moon

Your daddy won't be
home anytime soon.

behind enemy lines

My father child of war
went off to the jungle
came back a whore

He brought back his broken
body but behind enemy lines
he left his mind

And his soul too. He must
have seen something in the
light we couldn't see

He'd turn out the
lights and crunch ice in
the dark for hours

Until he left us
Stranded

Behind enemy lines

the Word

My words
are freedom words.
With words I set my Self free from forces unchecked
festering in old wounds, stagnate
in pools of my own bile

Words expand consciousness
Words connect and disconnect subconscious
With intellect

The new science of words
Words that change minds

In the beginning
was the Word and God said
And it was so. Everything became so from
Words spoken as
commands

Check
your words connect

your words with the mystical spiritual
Flow

And let it be so.

on meeting my muse

English cross on
Fishnet clad
Breasts

Silver earring through
Lips painted red like
Cherry Coke

Green eyes burn fierce
Like a trash can
On Fire

Black hair falls
Short on slender
Shoulders

Black dress mocks
The night hides the
Mystery of subtle hips

Black monster boots
Boosts height three

Inches taller

Painted green dragon
Breathes fire on
Back

Against skin like
Milk on a silk
Dress

She fades into the
Night like an ethereal
White ghost

people want to put me

In a box
Constrain the four corners
Of who I am
What they can't understand
Is I don't fit
                                            In a box

But that doesn't stop
Other people trying
Every which way the can
To stuff me
                                            In a box

I'd rather ride the waves
Of infinite possibilities
Exploring more realities
Than live
                                            In a box

If I think as small
As they want me to think
I'll be small enough

To fit

                                            In a box

But that's not for me

I guess some people
Are happy to live

                                              In a

Predictable
Small
Box.

a crack in the revolution

I imagine revolutions
start in coffee houses
like this one

Down a side street
in Pamplona, below ground
in a place that smells like history

No tourists or would be
writers here only
a merry band of brothers

Who vow to right
the social wrongs of society
through force of arms

A revolutionary makes
revolutions his highest
order of duty

Their fight is for the people
to redeem themselves against

the tyranny of evil men

Who are drunk with the
lust for power and control
and build them Selves up
on the backs of humble men

The guerrilla fighter travels
light for social reform

While I sit and stare
at the ass crack of the girl
who just sat down in front of me

Obscuring my view of the
revolution with a full on assault
against my modesty

And now...

Between sips of coffee and
revolution my eyes fall prey
to the horror of her ass crack
creeping out of her blue jeans

And I wonder...

Will this be the ass crack
that launched a thousand poets
to burn the topless towers of the oppressor?

The revolution awaits
I hear my call to arms
but first girl put a belt on
save the repressed!

chemical attraction

When I need a goodnight's sleep
I mix myself a cocktail
of chemicals

There's a couple of ways
to make the mix
either solo or in pairs

But by far
the sweeter brew
is that made by two

All you need is a little
up and down motion
a pinch of friction
and a dash of emotion

Add some heat
a bit of sweat
and some commotion

And in a minute or two

you'll get an explosion
the out fall of which
is a sweet mix of:

Norepinephrine
Seretonin
Oxytocin
Vas opressin
Nitric oxide
And prolactin

Next to heaven divine
all of these chemicals combine
to produce a goodnight's sleep

Warning: the effects have only
been proven to work on men
much to her chagrin

flight attendant

We whiz on the wings of
WizzAir, whizzing through
the air we breathe

Never mind our carbon footprint
we have to get from here to there
or go nowhere

I can't seem to get past
the air hostess's smudged
make-up, crooked nose
and venomous eyes

Perhaps she's served
to many coffees and creams
seen her dreams drift
up and down the same
old aisle two dozen times a flight

Or maybe she's just
A cold-hearted bitch
with a badge and pink shirt

and a smile that says:
I'd rather be anywhere than
in the air with you.

uber cool

I guess it's cool
To sit in an airport
Waiting for a cheap airline

In your black shoes
Black trousers
Black jumper
Black bag
Black watch
And yellow sunglasses

Only there's no sun
Inside the terminal

american girl

I wonder if this
girl will ever
shut up. She's been
talking non-stop
on our flight
up to Glasgow

The sound of the
propeller prop turning
cannot compete with
her high pitched squeal
and moaning

She's going on about
How the British
pronounce "Worcester"
and drive on the left
How they put milk
in their tea and call
their pants trousers
and cigarettes fags
How they speed down

the highway on a cold
sunny day with the top
down on the convertible
wrapped in their coats,
scarves and earmuffs
How they sit on the beach
in June with windbreaks
and jumpers turning
their noses to the rain

I'd like to stuff
a sock in her
mouth, or maybe a _____.
But that would be
rude and a little crude
even for her. Besides
which she'd probably
keep talking and later
pick me from her teeth.

So I best keep
my sock and
my _____ to myself
and pray the landing
gear works.

beast barracks

We were young
We were soldiers
We were proud

To be serving in the
Forces that guarded
Our way of life

You taught us the Law
And we learnt it well

Our shaved heads
Glistened in the sun
Like a hundred sweaty peaches
As we recited the Law:

Sir! The Law
We are not human
We are beasts
And you made us beasts
We will not talk
We will not sleep
We will not eat

Without permission
We will only dress
Right dress right dress
Ready front!

The last line is
Cold steel
Stick it between the
Second and third rib and twist!

is this the one

i came out of my
mother's womb like
i was here to stay

a smacked ass
and a snip made
me change my mind

now i pass my days
in pursuit of fine women
trying all i can to get
back inside

i know it's pointless
but i pray: let this one
be it for god's sake

and I give it another go

junk mail

We can make all your
secret wishes come true
women will go mad;
friends will be jealous:
a real man with a real
penis. Click <u>here</u> and have
the penis of you dreams.

We can give you what you
want – bigger penis, complete
with a law degree in the
we are not treating (the death
of MR Woolmer) as
come, fill your cup in the fire
of spring. Have they ever
told you this: (your

penis
is
really
tiny)?

Soft erection upon reflection
is less visually exciting;
less stimulating to your partner,
we can give you what you
want – start her day with
a bang and a buck and make
your dick massive.

how sweet she might smell

She is the perfect shade of pale
blonde and very white. Her dark
lined eyes stand out against her skin,
creating mystery in contrast to perfect
teeth, thin pink lips.

Her cleavage is as expansive
as snow covered fields and invite
my eyes to wander and my mind
to wonder about the joy between
two spaces, my heart paces.

She flicks her hair like pixie dust
casting spells on those near enough
to comprehend her beauty is only
skin deep but that is enough for me
as shallow as I am I would only drown
if there is more to her than I can see.

I care not what lies beneath her skin
the depth of her intellect would only
mean conversations I could do without.
Her voice is trapped behind glass while

I sit and stare from the shadows and smoke
pretending to be interested in A Theory of
Everything. What do philosophers know
of love and lust beyond wisdom's front?

I would rather have toast and tea and
contemplate how sweet she might smell
compared to a rose.

dr earnest and professor b

I

Professor B. knows the candle is burning
low
She confessed, stood, and watched him go

II

Freedom unleashed a flood of tears,
how many years had she been locked
away forced in the shadows while

Dr Earnest stole her life and her ambitions
A life sentence of promised love and
happiness
Forever, was more than she could bare to
pay

A promise she could not keep, a promise
made
on her behalf as Dr Earnest smiled and laid

the last brick leaving her to cower in the dark

III

But now she was free from all of that the open
road lay before her, wind in her hair, sun at her back, unlike Eve, she lacked the capacity

To deceive her lover anymore, she packed her
bags to go instead, in search of what she didn't
know, but hoped to find behind the rising sun

She quietly closed the door on predictability and
response, and watched her house, her home, her
life sink into the distance of her rear view mirror

IV

She sighed relief, pushed the petal to the floor
and headed for the beach to watch the bonfire roar

Epilogue

Eos waited by the side of the road
she was hitching a ride to see the tide
and watch them burn in effigy Dr Earnest
and her pride

They danced around the open flame
singing songs of praise, would the
gods of domesticity hold them to blame
for what they'd done, sacrificed a tidy
life of predictability and bore for the open
road and freedom to explore

jane doe

it's cool she said,
put your hand on
my thigh

ordinarily I would
comply, but you see
i don't know her name

she smiles, shifts in
her seat, asks: 'how
about my toe?'

i say, 'I don't know
is this a game?'

you're cute, she says
but just the same, can
you massage my back?

she moves her hair
aside to make room
for my hands

before long we're
in the sack, i still don't
know her name

she came just the same
called me a girl's name

shannon i think it was
or maybe heather

i forgot when she
broke out the leather

the things she did
with a feather made
me come like a cannon

the sun chases
the moon
from the sky

she slips on
her dress, kisses my
nipple and says

good-bye

i beg for more

too late

she closes
the door

i try to call her
but i don't know
her name

now I see her
everywhere, the
bus, the train
the crowded shops
and playing fields

she even turned up
once at a school recital
in a black bridal dress
made of leather with
strips of feathers
around her waist

now every girl i see
that looks like her i
want to run and ask:

are you the one
who left me in bed
rummaging through
every female name
in my head looking
for one that would fit
you?

they shake their heads
no and scurry away
in haste,

no wait, don't go
are you my jane doe?

song of my ancestors

(i)

The song of my ancestors
played in the wind as I stood
looking over the coast of West Africa

I felt, in the wind, a thousand
ancient fingers reading the coded
lines on my face, tracing the
roots of my history

I felt them squeeze my chin and
cheeks together the way my
Grandmother used to do when I
had not seen her in a season

'Boy you done grown,' she'd say
'You're my little man now.'

(ii)

In the ocean breeze, a family

reunion, faces I'd never seen
appeared before me in the sand
and surf and sky

I breathed deep their ancient
Wisdom and Knowledge, felt them
feasting on my soul and all at
once past and present became as one

I felt the history of my people and
the gifts they'd bestowed on the
Earth and the Moon, gifts that have
been forgotten, washed away in the
sea of time, trapped in sails of
black commerce

(iii)

The wind grew stronger
and the ocean pounded
an ancient rhythm
against the rocks

I watched my ancestors dance
around a fire in the sky and I

danced the dance too, the rhythm
hidden in my bones

and in one voice I heard them
sing above the ocean drums.

(iv)

The time for you is now young
warrior listen to hear, the ancient
rhymes and rhythms hidden in every
rock and tree, in a bird's wing flapping,
and the breaking of the sea.

The mysteries lie between and betwixt
The boundaries of light and shadow where
No-thing is nothing and one is one and
All alone, and evermore will be so.

(v)

And with that they were gone, the
past faded back into the sea and the
wind was calm again.

4. Whiskey Shots

torture

Notorious soldiers wore
Black uniforms, separated
Fathers, mothers, sisters,
And brothers; they had
No mercy

Prisoners interrogated.

Bodies disappeared one
By one; I was lucky –

I had no feelings.

death part I

Death hides behind every corner, every bend.
To some he is an enemy, to some he is a friend.
Death favors those who live in sin.
But he claims all in the end.

i think, therefore

I am
Thoughts
One small word
Eight letters yet
Everything I am
Therefore,

echo

I'm standing on the edge
of my mind killing time
before I fall into the black
pit and hear my silent scream
echo for eternity.

dawn

Up and about at dawn
I stretch and yawn
My head still groggy
Soggy from another late night
But I'm eager to write
So I say it's okay
And pick up my pen
Relax into Zen, the mystical flow
Receiving what the gods and the universe know

the shakes

I am a mass
of jumbled craziness
insanity sweeps over me
urging me somewhere forward
to a place I've never been, a road
I don't know. I've got the shakes
again and want to speed the journey to its

end.

coffee

coffee
the black magic
warms my heart, soothes my soul
takes me on journeys near and far
in cups.

self-portrait

Poet
laid-back and calm
writing meaningful words
flowing from zen into my pen
to share.

death part II

Death, he gets his gratification
By serving man his termination
And when all men meet their expiration
Death gives no explanation.

listen

tick tock

tick tock

listen to the sound of the clock.

that's your life ending one tick tock at a time.

5. A World Gone Mad

turn the page

i turn the page

depressed, the headlines have
me sinking in despair, is there
no way out, i am stressed

i turn the page

wall street took another blow
the dow hit a five year low
icelandic boss, shakes his head
says coolly, sorry for the billion dollar loss

i turn the page

i'm confused by the news
of banks that refuse to give
the people back their money,
this shit isn't funny, if it were
you or i, they'd take our homes
our cars, our color TV's
leave us living in the street
to beg, borrow, and steal
to make the ends meet

i turn the page

the words don't get any better,
investment banker stands before
congress, smiles like the Cheshire
Cat, he says i confess i made a fucking
mess and left the economy and the
taxpayer to discover they're in a
fucking quagmire from which they'll not
soon recover, i guess i'll retire,
live out my days flying across the airways,
from paris to milan to catch the ballets
with the money i took from the company
as i watched the MTHR FCKR
burn to the ground, while me and
the boys played another round

i turn the page

we've gone from economic enjoyment
to mass unemployment, pundits predict
millions of people will loose their jobs
victims of the meltdown, engineered by
a few clowns at the top of the hill
politicians think they can fix this with a bill

i turn the page

people are bracing for hard times
there's chaos in the stores, folks
rushing to buy cases of lager on
sale for a fiver so they can go home

and sit on the sofa and sulk and
watch reruns of MacGyver, they
make empty toasts to prosperity past
and hope the bad times won't last

i turn the page

stand together

The soldiers tossed the chicken
Bones, they didn't like his politics.
Strung him up on a cross and
Gambled for his ragged clothes.

Cancel the Second Coming,
The church has decreed, no
Heroic figure can save us
From our avarice, lust, and greed.

The twisted logic of confrontation
And violence are meant to be
Suffered in silence, let the ruthless
Gain at the expense of the poor,
It's what free markets were designed for.

The bishop takes the podium:
"Stand together," he shouts, "Or
We shall all hang separately in an
Economic bubble we can't sustain."

A dictator disposed in the gallows,
They didn't like his politics.
Strung a noose around his neck
Streamed his pictures across the Internet.

A mobile phone exposes the insanity

Of our tricked out humanity, evolved.

the guru

We bow our heads in quiet
servitude to the dust, our lips
form prayers to gods, who
long ago abandoned us.

We huddle together in a candle
lit room; frankincense, jasmine,
and sage, form broken patterns
in the air; amethyst rock, lapis lazuli,
crystal quartz, and rose guard the
four corners of the room, silent
sentries and witnesses to our gloom.

Here we try to replicate
perfect peace profound, but
how will we ever know peace
when we can't recall her name?

We close our eyes to quiet our
minds and search for peace
against the turmoil of the day.
Eirene begins to cry, she knows
we will not find her here
among these relics of the past.

The guru takes the mic.
He's seen the wondrous light

and has come to lead us there
to death's dream kingdom.

His words, mellow and sweet,
strokes the back of our necks
and lulls us to sleep, and deeper
we travel to death's other kingdom.

The guru licks his lips and passes
the offering plate around, let us pray!
The guru smiles, he knows we will
not see the light, how can we when
our eyes are closed?

prophet man

please mr prophet man
tell me what is true
I hear some say religion
is good for you

but i'm not sure
when in god's name
they tell me bombs
and bullets are the cure

The End